Hi! My name is Baby Loon!
Here I am—growing inside my beautiful speckled egg!

My mom sits on me
keeping me warm and
protecting me.

I already love her!

Mom and Dad
are patiently waiting for me to be born!

And, Hello,
Here I am!!

I was born on July 6th—almost a firecracker!!

I just love being on the water, swimming next to Mom, exercising, and just floating on a sunny day. It's so much fun out here!

Mom and Dad are always feeding me.
Look at this big crayfish!

I ate the WHOLE thing!

Mom is so nice
and lets me hide under her wing.

We travel as a family all the time!

Sometimes my parents need some adult time. I'm supposed to be very quiet to stay safe...

...but I like to splash and make bubbles!

I am so happy when Mom and Dad come back again.

Swimming is so much fun!

I'm getting
tiny feathers—
even around my eyes.

Look at me, I'm still mostly in my 'downy' stage.
Look at my cute li'l tail!

I just love spreading my new, black tipped wings...

...and flapping my big feet, one at a time. They are good for paddling around the lake. (Not by myself yet!)

My eyes are turning red
and I'm getting more feather definition.

I have to preen
and
clean myself to
loosen any downy
li'l fluffs that are
falling out.

Look at my bright
white belly!

I love to snuggle Mom's neck!

Mom still gets me great meals.

She gets more hugs, of course.

They show me how to search for food.

I'm learning to dive without a splash.

Remember when
I used to ride
on my mom?

Well now I'm big.
Sorry, Mom,
I don't need a ride
anymore. I'm pretty
strong and getting
stronger.

And here I am practicing my loon call.
It's still a li'l scratchy sounding,
but I'm proud of my new voice.

Oh boy.
Mom's teaching
me to take off.
I'd better pay
attention!

MOM! Look out—here I come!!

Fall is here!

OK, I'm ready to go!
Mom and Dad taught me
everything I need to know.
I can do this!!

Hey, this is fun running
across the water!

Well, it's September 27th and I'm going to explore.
Good bye—thanks for watching me grow!!